AF378687

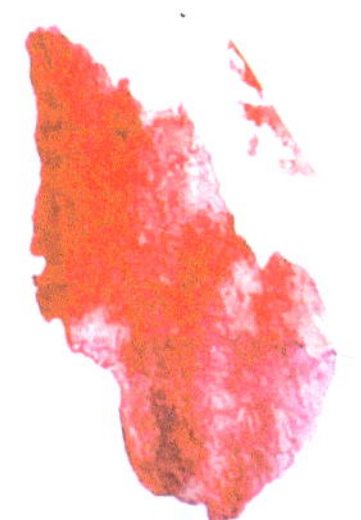
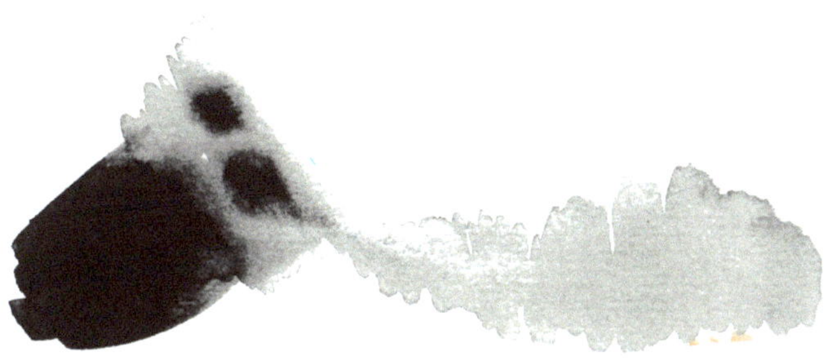

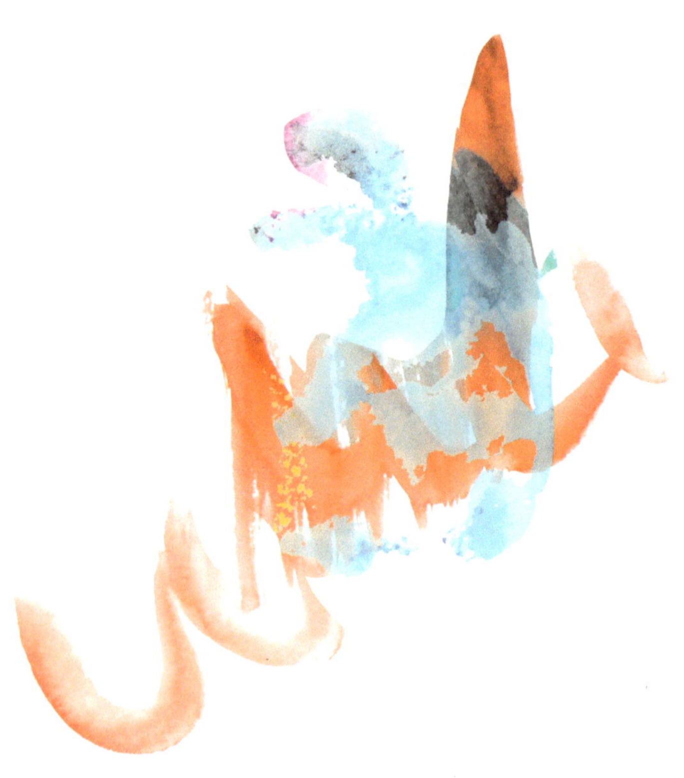

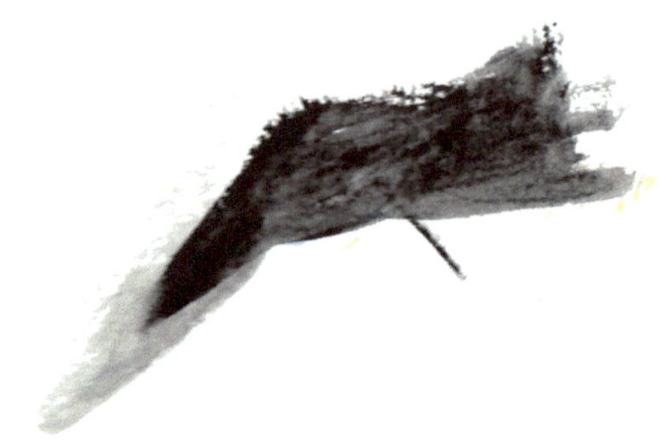

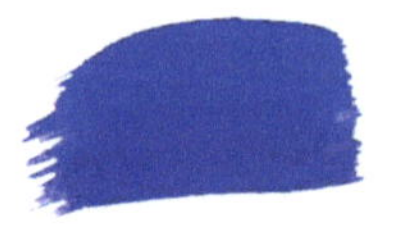

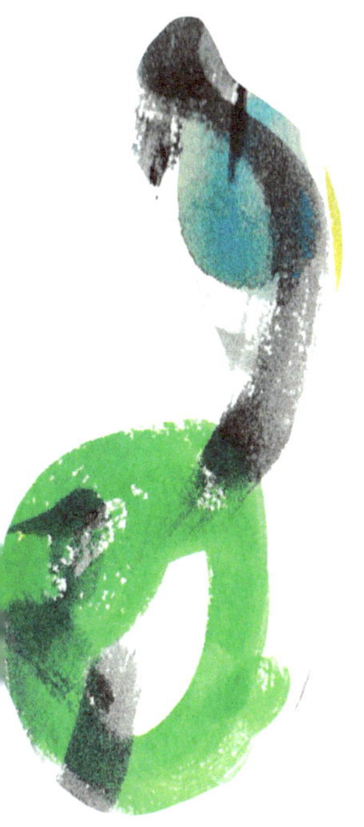

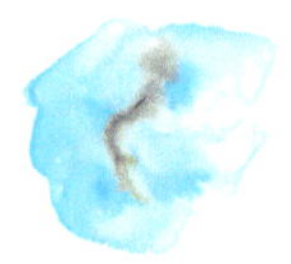

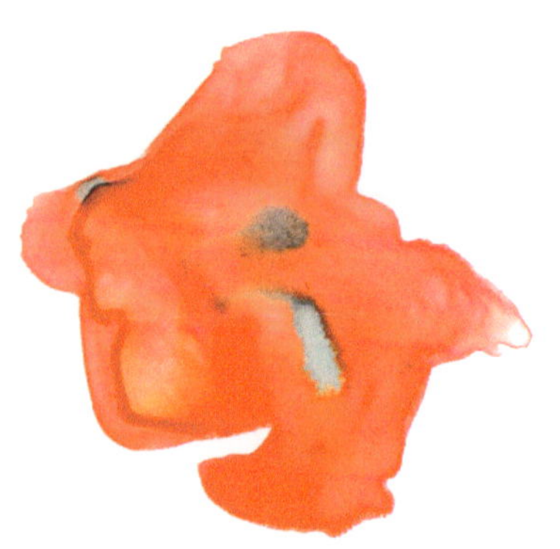

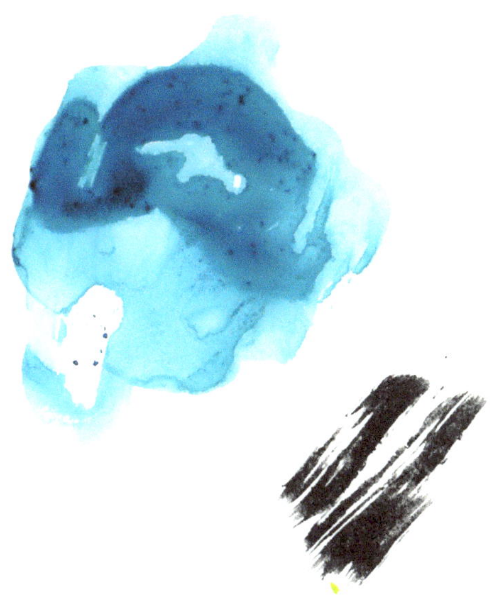
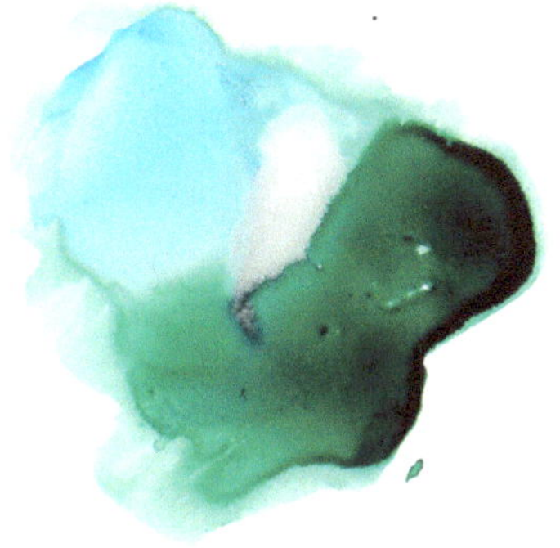

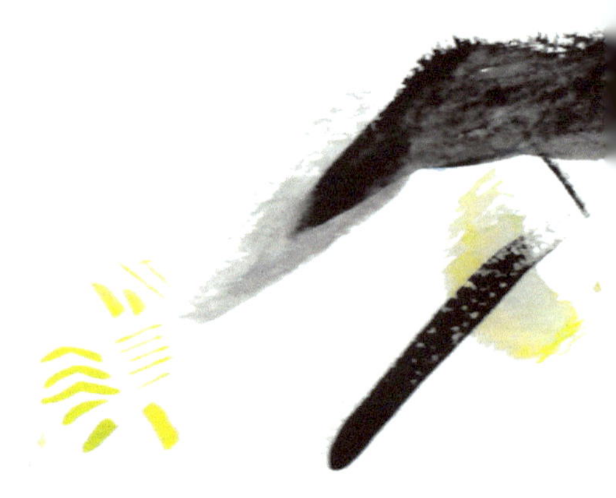

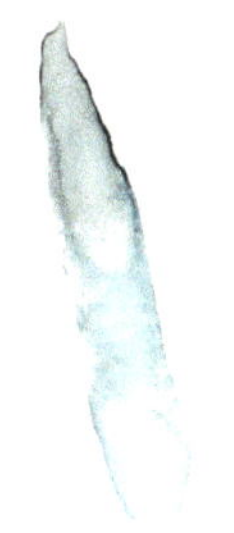
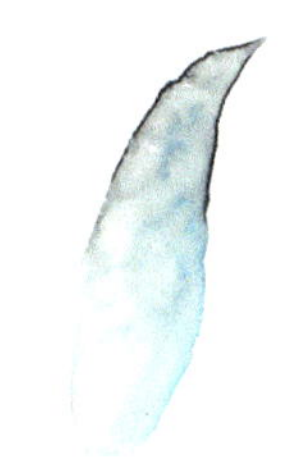
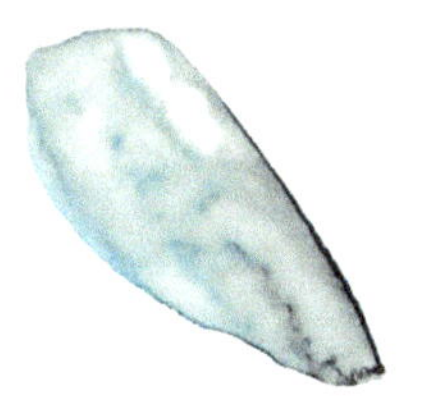

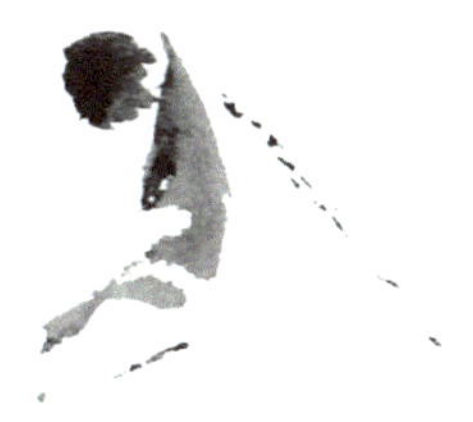

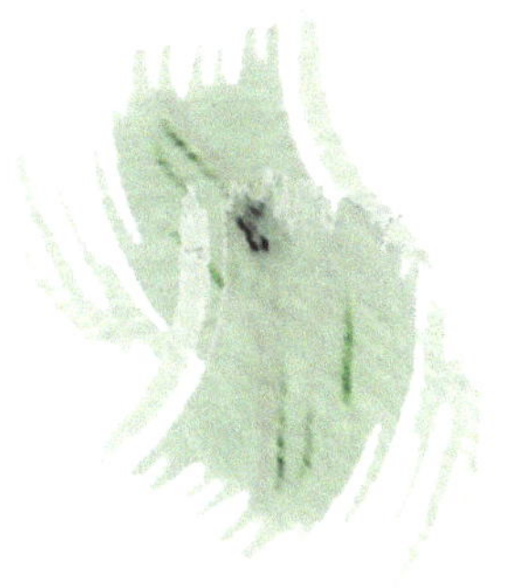

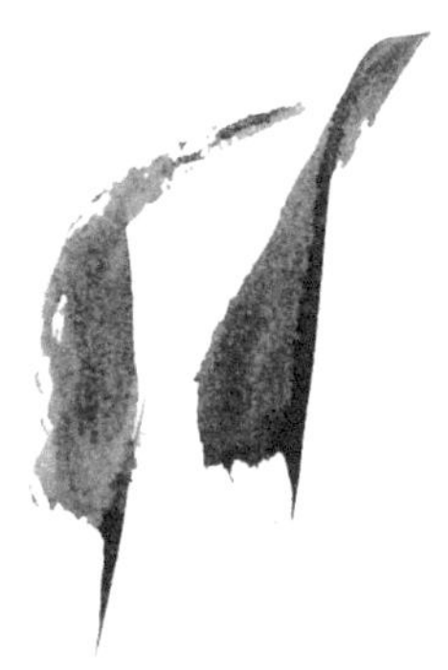

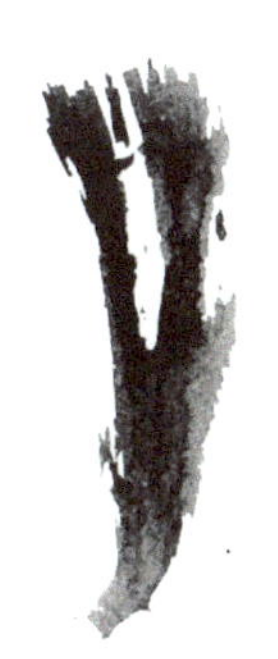

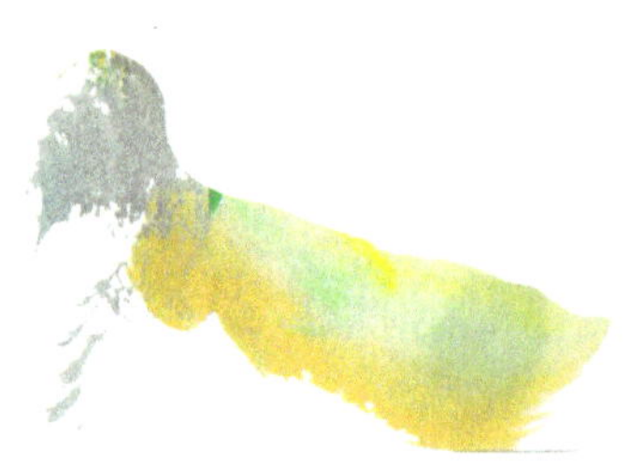

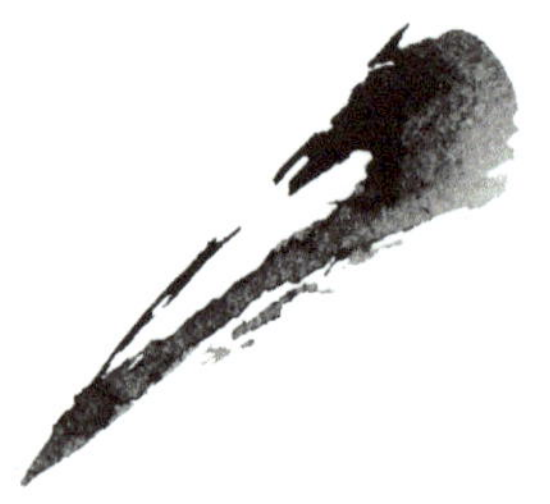

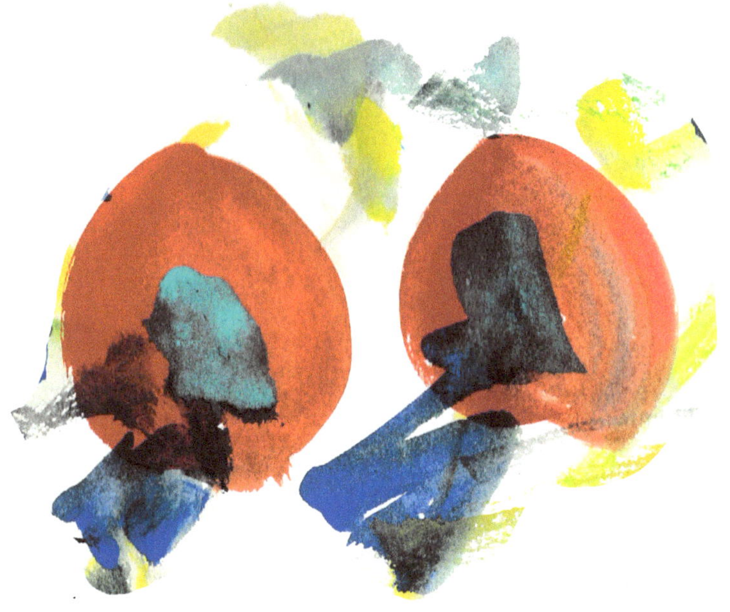

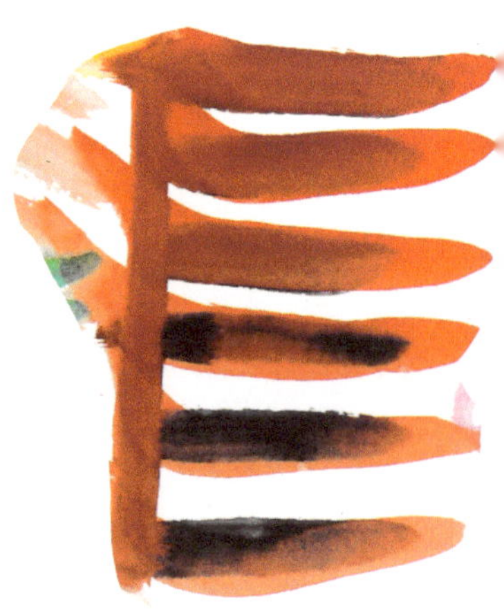

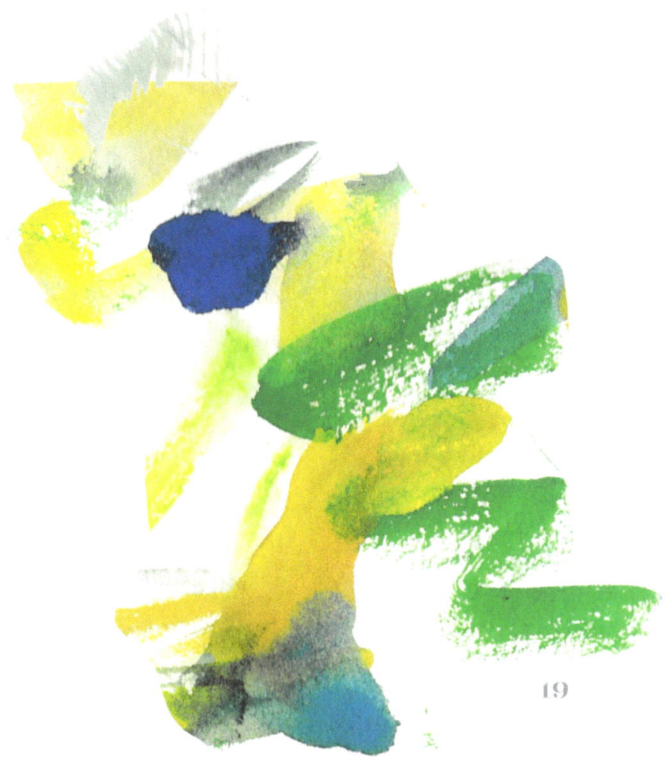

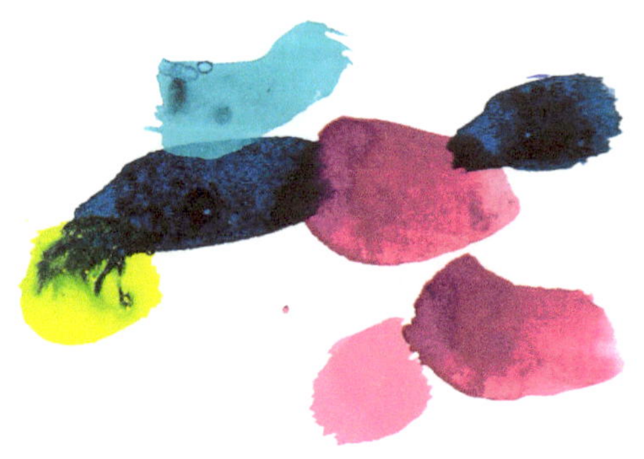

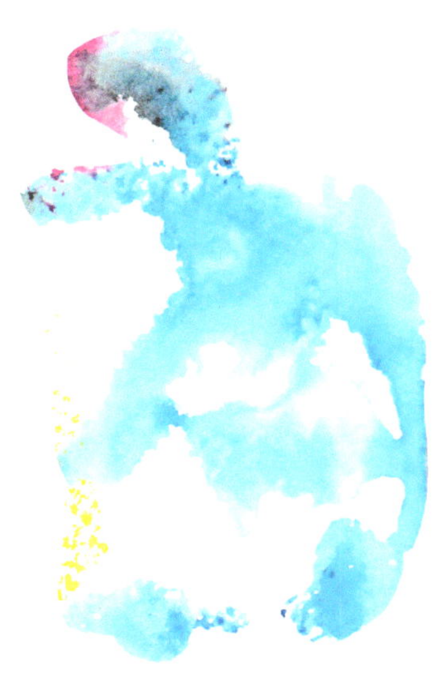

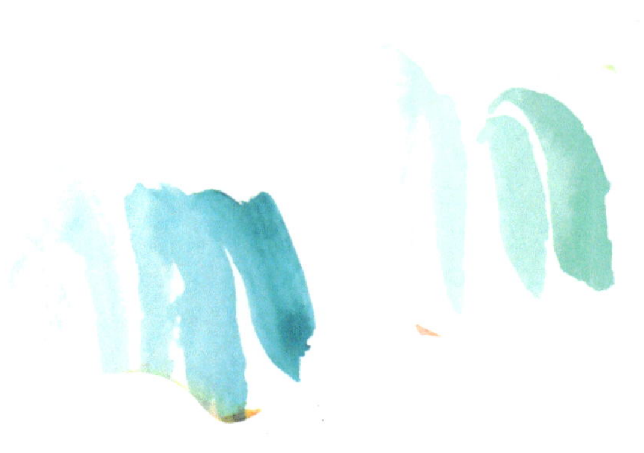

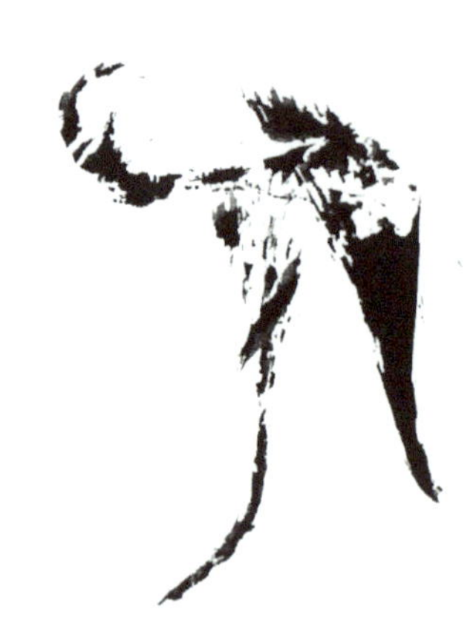

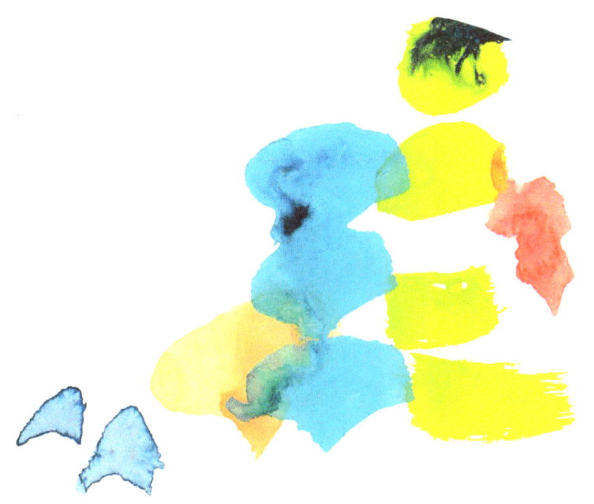

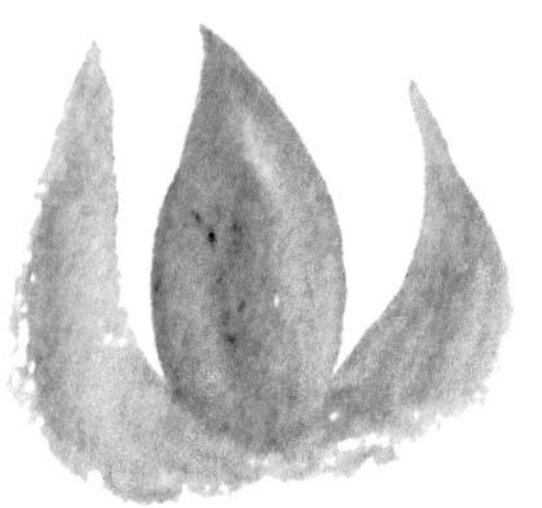

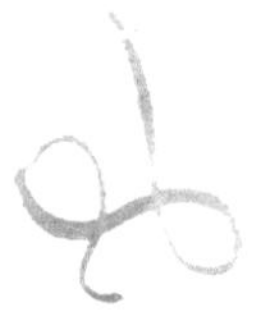

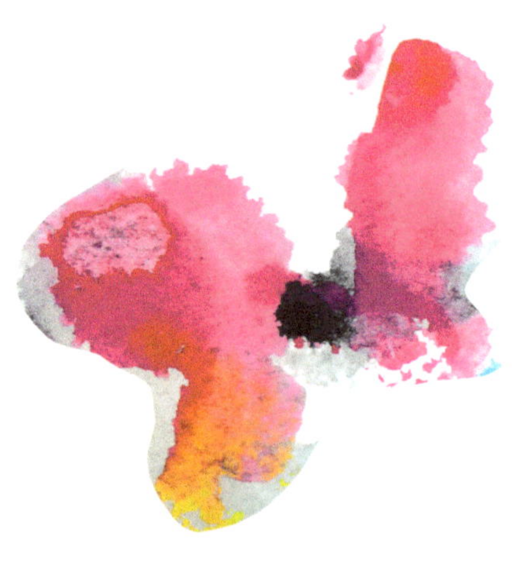

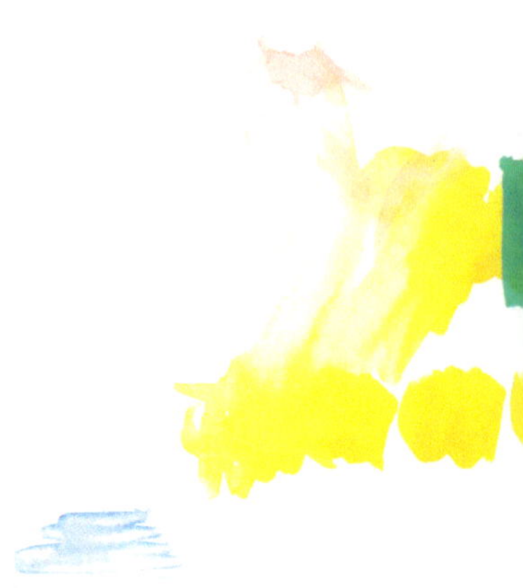

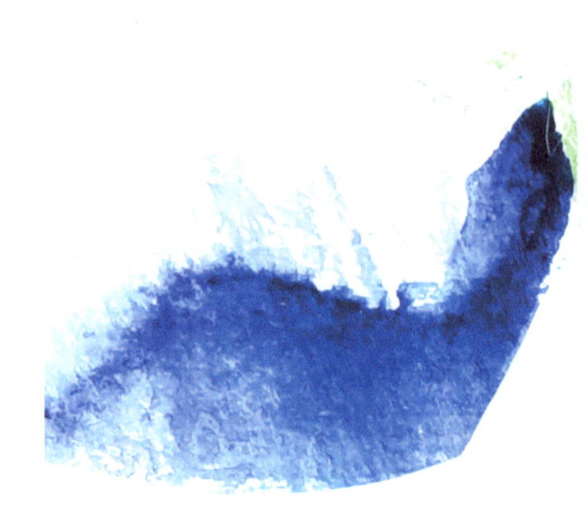

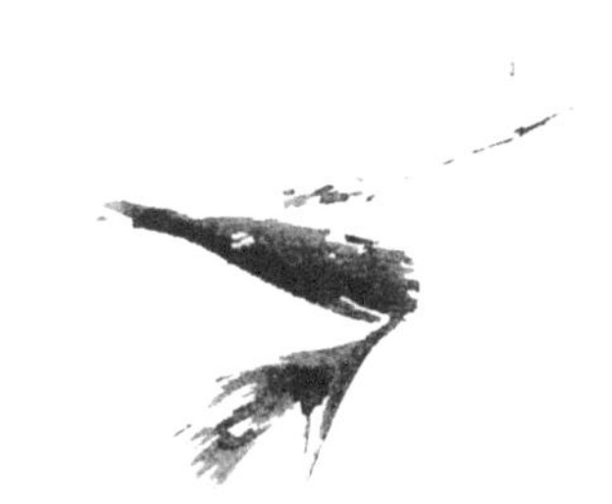

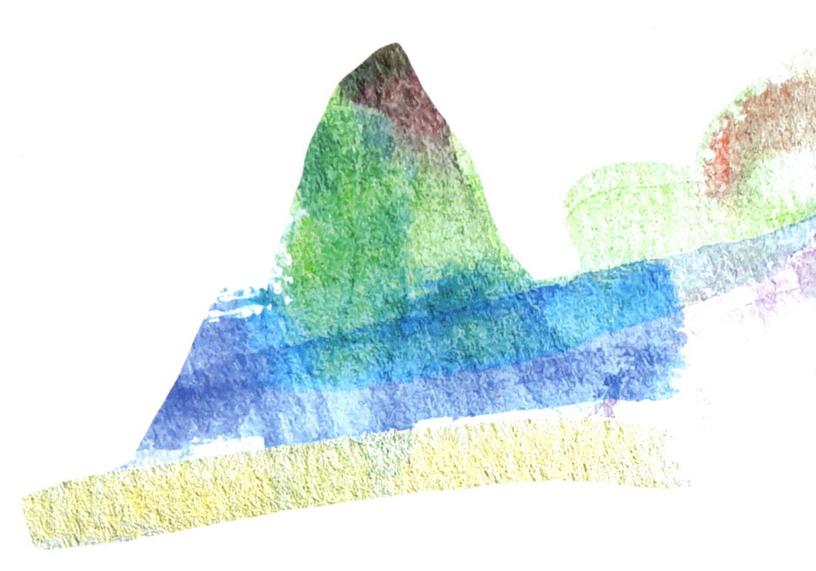

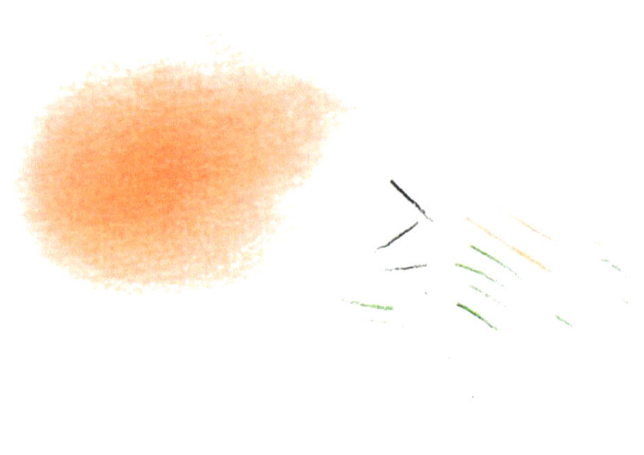

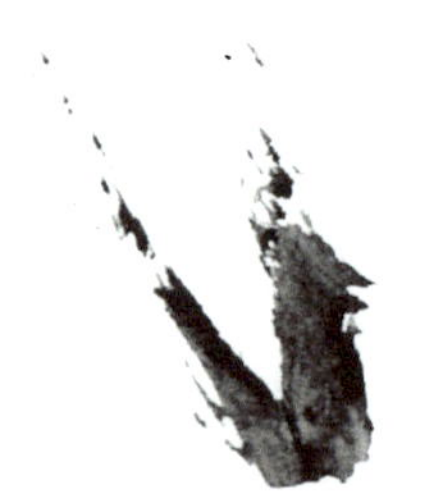

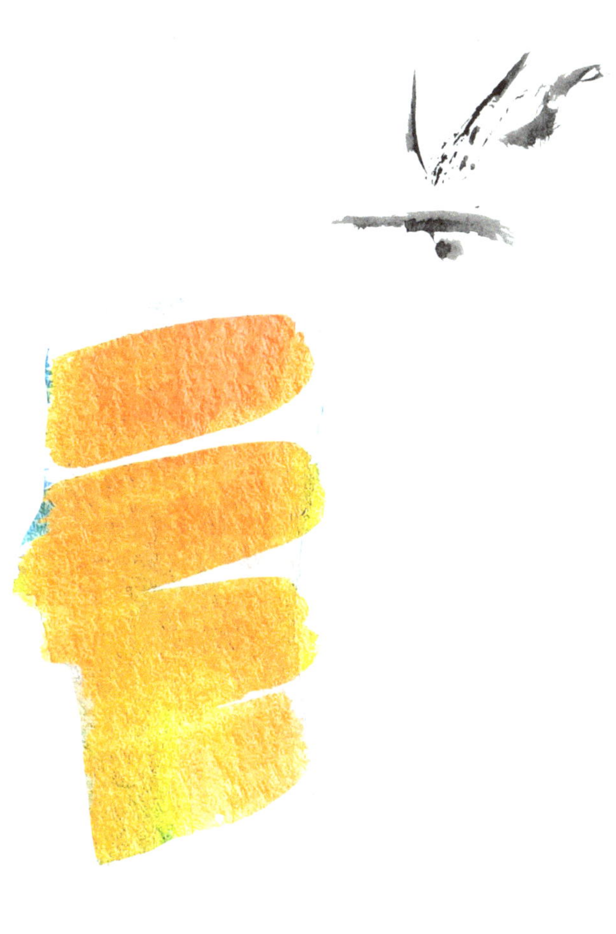

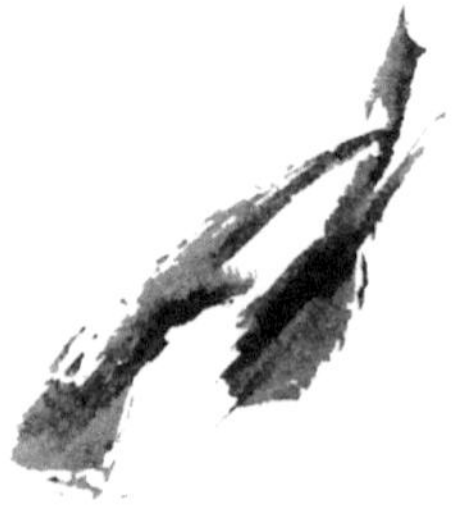

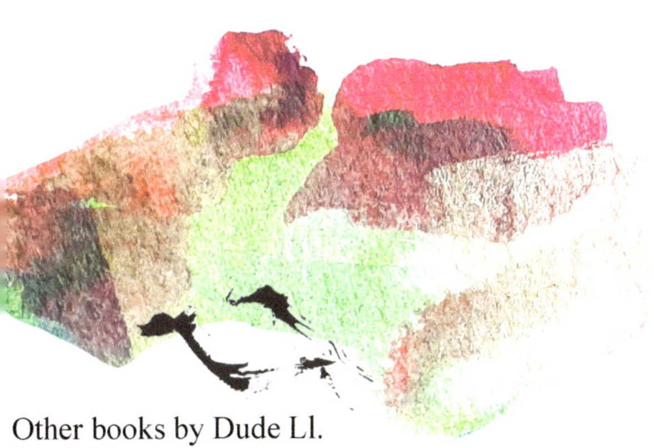

Other books by Dude Ll.
R.B.O.C Art prompt series.

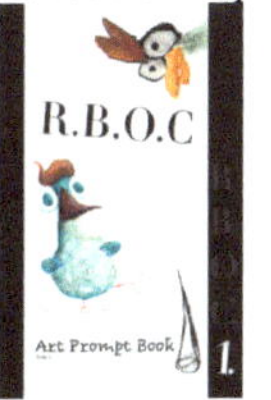
R.B.O.C #1 (B&W)
ISBN: 9781925991437

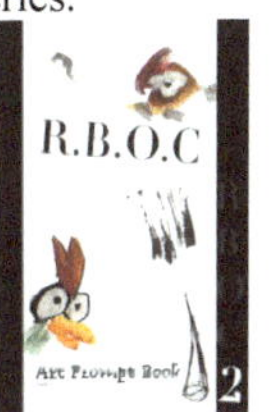
R.B.O.C #2 (B&W)
ISBN: 9781925991444

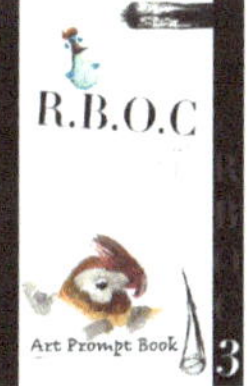
R.B.O.C #3 (B&W)
ISBN: 9781925991451

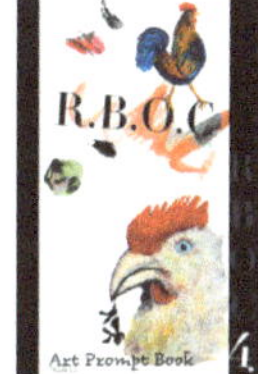
R.B.O.C #4 (Colour)
ISBN: 9781922415141

Doodle with Intent
A quirky picture book series for adults, (not X-rated or consecutive).
Available in hardcase and paperback.
More information @NoooBooks.

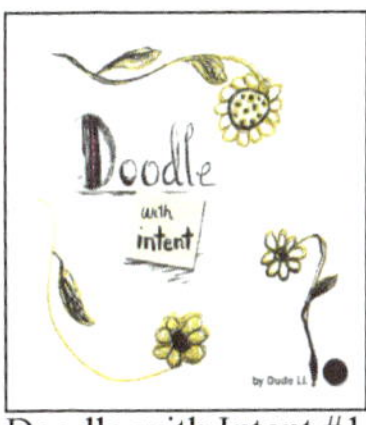
Doodle with Intent #1
ISBN: 9781925991505

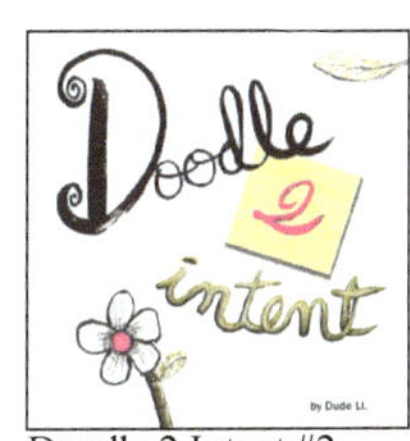
Doodle 2 Intent #2
ISBN: 9781925991819

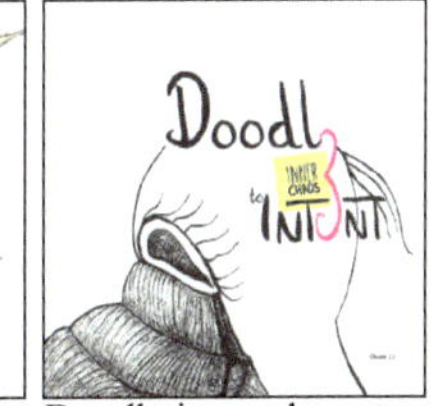
Doodle inner chaos to intent #3
ISBN: 9781922415059

CPSIA information can be obtained
at www.ICGtesting.com
Printed in the USA
LVHW070841290321
682811LV00004B/9